My Weird Reading Tips

Dan Gutman

Pictures by

Jim Paillot

HARPER

An Imprint of HarperCollinsPublishers

To Bria Ragin

The reading comprehension passages in this book were
excerpted from the following previously published books:

My Weirder School #7: Miss Kraft Is Daft! © 2012 by Dan Gutman; My Weirder School
#4: Mr. Burke Is Berserk © 2012 by Dan Gutman; My Weird School Fast Facts: Geography © 2016 by Dan Gutman; My Weirdest School #4: Mrs. Meyer Is on Fire! © 2016 by
Dan Gutman; My Weirder School #12: Mrs. Lane Is a Pain! © 2014 by Dan Gutman; My
Weirder School #6: Mayor Hubble Is in Trouble! © 2012 by Dan Gutman; My Weirdest
School #5: Miss Daisy Is Still Crazy! © 2016 by Dan Gutman; My Weirdest School #1:
Mr. Cooper Is Super! © 2015 by Dan Gutman; My Weirdest School #10: Miss Newman Isn't Human! © 2018 by Dan Gutman; My Weird School Fast Facts: Dinosaurs,
Dodos, and Woolly Mammoths © 2018 by Dan Gutman; My Weird School Daze #12:
Ms. Leakey Is Freaky! © 2011 by Dan Gutman; My Weirdest School #6: Mr. Nick Is a
Lunatic! © 2016 by Dan Gutman; My Weird School: Talent Show Mix-Up © 2016 by
Dan Gutman; My Weird School: Teamwork Trouble © 2018 by Dan Gutman; My Weird
School Goes to the Museum © 2016 by Dan Gutman; My Weirdest School #8: Mrs.
Master Is a Disaster! © 2017 by Dan Gutman; My Weirdest School #12: Ms. Hall Is a
Goofball! © 2018 by Dan Gutman

The author gratefully acknowledges the editorial contributions of Bridget Heos.

My Weird Reading Tips

ISBN 978-0-06-288239-4 (pbk. bdg.)—ISBN 978-0-06-288240-0 (library bdg.)

19 20 21 22 23 PC/BRR 10 9 8 7 6 5 4 3 2 1
❖
First Edition

Contents

Introduction

My name is Dan, and I hate reading.

Well, I *used to* hate it, anyway. When I was a kid in second and third grade, I didn't like to read. My parents weren't happy about that, of course. Both of them were big readers. There were lots of books around the house. My mom and dad were reading all the time, it seemed. So was my older sister, Lucy. But not me.*

Like a lot of kids, I found reading to be hard to do. It was *hard* to put the letters together to make words. It was hard to fit

---

*Why are you reading this? The story is up there!

the words into sentences that made sense, the sentences into paragraphs, and the paragraphs into chapters. It wasn't any fun for me. It was work, and it was boring work. I would rather be outside playing baseball, or riding my bike.

But at some point, I changed my mind. I *got* it. Reading didn't *have* to be boring. It could be fun. It was like a light switch turned on and the room wasn't dark anymore.

Today I love to read, and I read just about all the time.

 I hope he doesn't read while he's in the shower. That would be weird.

My mother was amazed when I grew up and became a professional writer. Now, wherever I go, I take a book, a magazine, or a newspaper with me in case I have a spare moment to catch up on my reading. I like to learn new stuff.

I'll tell you what changed things for me—sports. I was a big baseball fan as a kid. I rooted for the New York Mets (and still do). I wanted to find out more about baseball. When I was a kid, believe it or not, you couldn't go online and just google anything you wanted to know about. It wasn't that easy. Google didn't exist. The Internet didn't exist. In fact, personal computers and cell phones didn't even exist!

That must have been a million hundred years ago.

Can you imagine what life was like in those prehistoric times? When I was a kid and I wanted to find out about something, I had to *read* about it. My parents had a complete set of the *Encyclopedia Britannica* on a shelf in the living room, and a big, thick dictionary. But more often than not, I had to go to the library.

So I gobbled up books, magazines, and newspaper articles about baseball and other sports. I memorized the statistics on the back of my baseball cards. And slowly but surely, I discovered that reading was fun *when I was reading about something that interested me*. To this day, I find it hard to read things that don't interest me. It's hard to concentrate.

I know that a lot of kids out there don't like reading, just like me. Maybe you try to avoid it. Maybe you just refuse to do it. But let's get real. You're going to have to do a lot of reading in your life, whether you like it or not. Street signs. Texts from your friends. Maps. Emails. Instruction manuals. Even if you never pick up a book, words are all around you. It's a skill we all have to learn.

So this book is for all you kids out there who claim you hate to read. You really don't. You just haven't found the book that turns on that light switch. But it will happen. And you know what? You may just discover that reading is fun!

Cheers,

Dan Gutman

P.S.: Oh, by the way, this book isn't going to be some boring lesson that just teaches you how to read better. It will include tips and activities to help you improve your reading skills, but it's not a lecture. It's a My Weird School book! Even if you're a fan of the series, you probably don't even realize all the ways that you're becoming a better reader when you read a My Weird School book. But A.J., Andrea, and I are going to tell you the secrets of My Weird School.

Shhhhh! Don't tell anybody. Ready? Let's go!

 Reading tip from Andrea: My name is Andrea, and I LOVE reading! While you read this book, I'm going to chime in every so often when I have a little tip that might help you with your reading. Talk to you soon!

Just ignore her!

Chapter I:

Main Idea and Supporting Details

Very often, confused readers will email me and ask, "Why did you write _____? It makes no sense." Or "Why did you put _____ in the story?"

Usually, there's a good reason for anything that happens in the story. It moves the story forward. It explains something you need to know. It sets up something that's going to happen later.

But sometimes, I must admit, there's no good reason. I just put stuff in the book because I thought it was funny and I wanted to make you laugh.

And I don't think there's anything wrong with that. If the reader is laughing and keeps turning the pages, that's a good enough reason to include something in the story.

Still, every paragraph or story has a **main idea**. And it's important to be able to spot it, because knowing the main idea will help you understand what a paragraph or a story is really about.

In the My Weird School series, the main idea of each book is usually that a new grown-up has come to the school for one reason or another, and the story will revolve around that person. The main idea usually doesn't appear until Chapter 2, 3, or 4. In *Miss Kraft Is Daft!*, for example, the first chapter is about Mr. Granite and his head full of snot. I did that for a simple reason—*to get him out of the way*. The book is about Miss Kraft, his substitute teacher. If you're going to have a sub, the regular teacher can't be around, of course. So I gave Mr. Granite a cold in Chapter 1 so Miss Kraft could replace him in Chapter 3.

And, of course, snot is funny. Milk coming out of your nose is even funnier.* But "snot" is a lot funnier than "mucus."

---

*Come to think of it, just about *anything* that comes out of your nose is funny.

Reading tip from Andrea: Got nothing to do? Go to the public library (it's free!) or your local bookstore. You never know what treasures you'll find there.

It Takes Brains to Be a Sub

Read this passage from *Miss Kraft Is Daft!*, which is told from A.J.'s point of view, then use it to complete the activities that follow.

You know what it means when your teacher gets sick? It means you get a *substitute* teacher!

Yay!

Having a sub is cool, because you don't have to do work or learn anything. You can do whatever you want. It's too bad teachers can't be sick *all* the time. Then school would be fun.

I pulled out a comic book and put my feet up on my desk. This was going to be the greatest day of my life.

But you'll never believe who ran into the door at that moment.

It was a lady dressed up like a clown and riding a unicycle! She ran right into the door!

"Ouch!" said the clown lady as she got up off the floor. "That hurt!"

Everybody laughed, because it's always hilarious when people crash into things and fall down. Nobody knows why.

If you ask me, there should be a TV station that shows nothing but people crashing into things and falling down all day long. That would be cool.

"Hi boys and girls!" the clown lady said. "My name is Miss Kraft."

"Are you a clown, or a teacher?" asked Andrea.

"Both!" said Miss Kraft. "I'm a clown *and* a teacher. We're going to have fun and learn at the same time!"

All About Subs

The **main idea** is the most important thought in a paragraph, passage, or story. It's what the whole text is really about. **Supporting details** provide more information about the main idea. Sometimes they explain why the main idea is thought to be true.

Directions: Which of these four sentences is the main idea of the passage you just read? Circle your answer below or write it on a separate sheet of paper.

1. a. A.J.'s class is getting a substitute teacher.

b. Today is going to be the greatest
day of A.J.'s life.

c. Having a sub is cool.

d. Miss Kraft is both a clown and a
teacher.

Directions: In the space below or on a separate sheet of paper, fill in the blanks in these supporting details with words from the passage.

2. If your teacher gets _____,
then you get a substitute teacher.

3. A.J. thinks having a sub is cool,
because you don't have to do
_____ or learn anything.

4. A.J. pulls out a _____ and
puts his feet on the desk.

5. The lady who runs into the door is
riding a _____.

Just for Laughs

Not every detail in a passage supports the main idea. Some details are there for other reasons. They may be there just to make you laugh.

Directions: In the space below or on a separate sheet of paper, write **yes** if the detail supports the main idea "A.J.'s class is getting a substitute teacher,"* and **no** if it does not.

1. A.J. says having a sub is cool. _____

2. A.J. thinks that he can do whatever he wants when he has a substitute. _____

*Oops, we gave you the answer to the first question in the book.**
Oops, all answers are given at the back of the book anyway, so this wasn't an actual oops.*
***This oops was the real oops.

3. It's always hilarious when people crash into things and fall down. _____

4. Miss Kraft is both a clown and a teacher. _____

Gross and Mysterious

Directions: In the space below or on a separate sheet of paper, write a paragraph about a time when your class had a substitute teacher, using the main idea provided. Include at least three supporting details. You may also include a sentence that's just for fun!

Main Idea: One time, my class had a substitute teacher.

_____

_____

_____

_____

_____

_____

_____

Reading tip from Andrea: When you sit down to read, turn off the TV. Turn off the music. Hide your phone, if you have one. Go to a place where you can't hear people talking. All those things are distracting and make it hard to concentrate.

Chapter 2:

Summarizing a Story

When it's time for me to work on a new My Weird School book, I don't just write any old thing that pops into my head. First, I write a short summary—a few sentences—and run that by my editor to get his approval. An editor is a person at a publishing company who works with authors to make sure their books are as good as they can possibly be.

Here's the summary from *Ms. Hall Is a Goofball!* . . .

"Ms. LaGrange is leaving, and that

means there's a new lunch lady at Ella Mentry School. But when Ms. Hall makes it her mission to get A.J. and the gang to eat more veggies, they form a club to protest. Will Ms. Hall be able to lure them over to the veggie side? Or will their resistance be a piece of cake?"

That summary, you may have noticed, appears on the back cover of the book.

Where do the ideas come from? It's not the genius of my creative brain.

 That's for sure!

It's a process. I'm sure you've noticed that each My Weird School book focuses on a different grown-up at Ella Mentry School. So when the series started, I made a list of grown-ups who work in schools— the principal, the art teacher, the music teacher, the custodian, and so on. After I choose the person I'll be writing about, I brainstorm about that job and try to think of funny situations that person might be in.

For example, I didn't really know what speech teachers do, so when I wrote *Miss Laney Is Zany!*, I contacted a few speech teachers and interviewed them. The same with *Miss Klute Is a Hoot!* I didn't know what therapy dogs do, so I interviewed several trainers to get ideas I could use in the story.

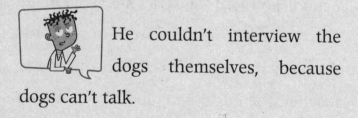 He couldn't interview the dogs themselves, because dogs can't talk.

I'll give an example to show you how the

process works. Custodians, as you know, often have to clean up the messes that kids make at school. That must be really hard work. So for *Miss Lazar Is Bizarre!*, I thought it would be funny to have a custodian who *loves* to clean up messes. If there were no messes, she wouldn't have a job.

Messes often involve the bathrooms. Bathrooms are funny. Toilet bowls are even funnier. And toilet bowl plungers are *hilarious*. So I decided to have Miss Lazar create a museum of toilet bowl plungers. Then, at the end of the story, she would use a toilet bowl plunger to save Mr. Klutz's life when he has a panic attack. Once I had that idea, writing the rest of the story was a piece of cake.

What does cake have to do with toilet bowl plungers?*

It's a figure of speech, A.J.

Let's summarize! In Chapter 1, you learned how to find the main idea of a passage. When you summarize something, you describe what you read using fewer words. Here's an idea: Take a My Weird School book and try to summarize it for the back cover.

 I thought summarize meant to get your house ready for the summer.

---

*And why is everybody always talking about cake?

Uh, no.

Reading tip from Andrea: Read with a friend or a group of friends. You read one page, and your friend reads the next one. Talk about what you're reading. It's fun!

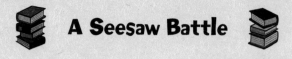

A Seesaw Battle

Read the chapter from *Mr. Burke Is Berserk!* in which A.J. watches a lawn mower race between school groundskeeper Mr. Burke and Principal Klutz. Then use it to complete the activities that follow.

The lawn mower race was hilarious because lawn mowers go *really* slow. I mean, I can *walk* faster than those things. It was like watching a turtle race. But it was still exciting, and everybody was yelling and screaming.

"Put the pedal to the metal, Mr. Klutz!"

"You can beat him, Mr. Burke!"

We all walked alongside the lawn mowers so we could see who was winning. First Mr. Klutz took the lead. Then Mr. Burke took the lead. Then Mr. Klutz was ahead. Then Mr. Burke was ahead.

"This is a real seesaw battle!" shouted Ryan.

"Are they going to fight on the seesaws?" I asked. "That would be *cool*!"

After about a million hundred minutes, the lawn mowers reached the other end of the playground. Mr. Burke jumped off and

touched the monkey bars first.

"Yee-ha!" he shouted. "Ah'm a-grinnin' like a weasel in a henhouse."

Mr. Klutz gave Mr. Burke a dollar. All the excitement was over, and we had to go into school to start the day. Bummer in the summer!

"Mr. Burke is weird," I said as we walked to class.

"Remember the time he grew a corn maze on the soccer field?" asked Neil.

"Remember the time he mowed big circles in the

30

grass and told us they were made by UFOs?" asked Michael.

"Maybe Mr. Burke isn't really a grounds-keeper at all," I said. "Maybe he kidnapped the real groundskeeper and locked him in the equipment shed where he keeps the lawn mowers. Stuff like that happens all the time, you know."

"Stop trying to scare Emily," said Andrea.

"I'm scared," said Emily.

"Mr. Burke probably escaped from a looney bin," said Ryan.

"Yeah," I said. "He probably snatches kids during recess and buries them under the monkey bars."

"We've got to *do* something!" Emily

shouted. Then she started freaking out and went running down the hallway.

Sheesh, get a grip! That girl will fall for *anything*.

Sum It Up!

A **summary** is a short description of a longer passage. While the main idea tells you what a passage or story is *mostly* about, a good summary will include specific supporting details from throughout the passage.

Directions: Using the space below or a separate sheet of paper, write a three- to five-sentence summary about what happened in the chapter you just read.

_____

_____

_____

Sum Up the Summary

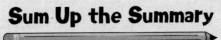

Directions: Can you write an even shorter summary of the chapter? In the space below or on a separate sheet of paper, write one or two sentences about the chapter. Include an illustration to go with it.

_____

_____

_____

Reading tip from Andrea: Find a comfy chair, couch, or a big pile of pillows to sit on while you read. Have a good, strong light over your shoulder. Sometimes I like to read outdoors, under a tree or lying on the grass.

Deserts

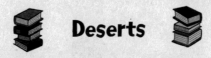

Read this passage from the nonfiction book *My Weird School Fast Facts: Geography*. Then use it to complete the activities that follow.

One third of the land on Earth is desert, and every one of the seven continents has at least one of them.

Do you know the difference between a desert and a dessert? A desert is any place that gets less than ten inches of rain or snow a year. A dessert is a tasty treat you have at the end of a meal. If I had the choice between being stranded in a desert or stranded in a dessert, I would definitely choose the dessert. At least you get something to eat.

 The biggest desert in the world is . . . the Sahara in North Africa, right?

Wrong! According to the definition of a desert, the largest one in the world is in Antarctica! I'll bet your parents don't know that.

The Sahara is the biggest sub-tropical desert. It stretches across eleven countries. But it's not the sandy desert you're thinking of. It's only 30 percent sand. The rest is rocky and mountainous.

The Arabian Desert on the Arabian Peninsula is the world's largest sand desert. There's another desert on the Arabian Peninsula called the Empty Quarter that is nothing but sand dunes. It's about the size of France.

Just Deserts

Directions: In the space below or on a separate piece of paper, fill in the blanks to summarize the passage. Use the words in the box.

rain   snow   sand   Antarctica

Sahara   continents

A desert is a place that gets less than ten inches of _____(1) or _____(2) a year. One third of the land on Earth is desert, and every one of the seven _____(3) has at least one desert. The largest desert in the world is in _____(4), but the biggest subtropical desert is the _____(5), and the Arabian Desert is the largest _____(6) desert.

A Little Bit Shorter Now

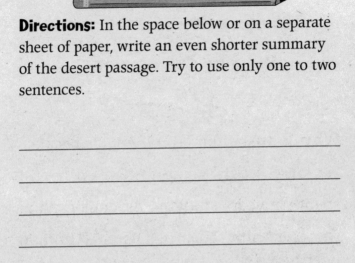

Directions: In the space below or on a separate sheet of paper, write an even shorter summary of the desert passage. Try to use only one to two sentences.

_____

_____

_____

_____

Chapter 3:

Making Predictions and
Drawing Conclusions

Why do we get bored? Often, it's because we know what's going to happen next. I spent six years studying psychology, and the one thing I learned is that human beings get used to things *really* quickly. Stories that are predictable are boring. We need almost constant novelty to keep us interested.

When you jump into a pool, you feel really cold for the first minute or so, but soon you don't feel cold anymore. When we get used to any situation, it becomes less interesting, and it can get to be boring. But if something new, exciting, and different is introduced, we get interested all over again.

Have you ever heard the term "cliffhanger"?

 Sure. That's when you hang off a cliff. So it has the perfect name.

Actually, A.J. is right. Back in 1873, the author Thomas Hardy wrote a book that ended with a character hanging off a cliff. Readers had to read the next book in the series to find out what happened. Authors do this sort of thing all the time. We want you to keep turning the pages, so we end the book (or a chapter) with a "cliffhanger." I often end My Weird School chapters with . . .

That's when the weirdest thing in the history of the world happened.

But I'm not going to tell you what it was.

Okay, okay, I'll tell you. But you have to read the next chapter. So nah-nah-nah boo-boo on you!

Human beings are curious creatures. As we read, it's natural for us to wonder what's going to happen next. It may feel like you're just scanning the words on the page, like a machine, but you're not. Your brain is processing the story, trying to predict where it's going. That's a good thing. If we didn't plan ahead, we wouldn't survive as a species.

But if I do my job right, the thing that happens next in the story won't be too predictable. It will be something new and different to get you interested in the story again. Also, there should be a surprise ending in the last chapter that wraps everything up.

After writing sixty My Weird School books, it's hard to surprise you kids with something you haven't read before. But I always try.*

---

*You should be on the edge of your seat reading this chapter. But you can sit anywhere you'd like.

Reading tip from Andrea: You don't have to read the whole book in one sitting. Read in bite-size chunks. Set a goal. Try to read one chapter. Or one page. Take a break after you reach your goal. Reward yourself.

A Real Spy Mission

Mrs. Meyer Is on Fire! is about a fire safety expert who the students think is not a real firefighter. They follow her to the firehouse to spy on her. Read this passage, told from A.J.'s point of view, then use it to complete the activities that follow.

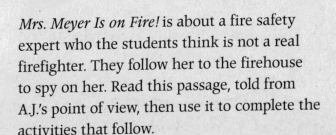

At that moment lights started flashing. Sirens started screaming. Bells started ringing. Whistles started blowing. Alarms started sounding. My ears started hurting.

"It must be a fire!" shouted Ryan. "We gotta get outta here!"

But it *wasn't* a fire. If it was a fire, all the firefighters would have jumped on the fire truck and driven out of the firehouse. Instead, they all jumped out from behind the fire truck and yelled at Mrs. Meyer . . .

"SURPRISE!"

A giant banner came down from the ceiling. . . .

"It's not a fire," said Michael. "It's Mrs. Meyer's birthday!"

"They're throwing her a surprise party!" said Andrea. "That's so sweet!"

Andrea was right for once in her life. All the firefighters gathered around Mrs. Meyer. They were hugging her and giving her presents.

"So I guess she really is a firefighter after all," said Alexia.

Well, we had accomplished our spy mission. We were about to turn around and go home. But that's when the most amazing thing in the history of the world happened.

"What are you kids doing here?" Mrs. Meyer suddenly asked.

She had spotted us! I didn't know what

to say. I didn't know what to do. I had to think fast.

"We . . . uh . . . came to wish you a happy birthday," I said.

"Great!" said Mrs. Meyer. "You're just in time for the party!"

Mrs. Meyer took us inside the firehouse and introduced us to all the other fire-fighters. They let us climb on a fire truck, which was really cool. And we got to pet their fire dog. But the coolest part was when they took us up to the second floor and let us slide down the fire poles. That was so much more fun than taking the stairs. I'm going to get my parents to put a fire pole in our house.

Emily was too scared, but the rest of us slid down the fire poles a million hundred times. Then one of the firefighters wheeled in a giant cake.

Cake! I love cake!

"This will make up for the cake I didn't get to eat on *my* birthday," said Emily.

Mrs. Meyer must be really old, because that cake had a *lot* of candles on it. Two of the firefighters lit them, and then we all sang "Happy Birthday."

"Make a wish," one of the firefighters told Mrs. Meyer.

She closed her eyes. That's when the weirdest thing in the history of the world happened.

Collecting the Evidence

A **prediction** is a guess as to what will happen next in a story or passage. A good prediction is based on **evidence** from the text. Evidence can be anything from the details in the story to the illustrations or even the title.

Directions: In the space below or on a separate sheet of paper, fill in the blanks with clues from the passage that will help you to predict what happens next in the story.

1. The title of the book is _____.

2. A birthday _____ was hanging up over the cake.

3. The birthday cake had lots of _____.

4. A.J. says, "That's when the _____ thing in the history of the world happened."

5. Since firefighters promote fire safety and put out fires, it would be *weird* for a fire to start at a _____.

Making Predictions

Directions: Read the predictions below. In the space provided or on a separate sheet of paper, write **yes** if the prediction is something that *could* happen next based on evidence from the story. Write **no** if the prediction is not based on evidence from the story.

1. While blowing out the candles, Mrs. Meyer's hair will catch on fire. ____

2. While blowing out the candles, "Mrs. Meyer" will pull off her mask and reveal herself to be Miss Daisy. ____

3. While Mrs. Meyer's eyes are closed, the firefighters' pet fire dog will run up and eat a piece of the birthday cake. ____

4. When a fire starts at the party, Emily will bravely slide down the fire pole and offer to put out the fire all by herself. __

What Comes Next?

Directions: Based on evidence from the passage, can you predict which of these three options will **most likely** happen next? Circle your answer or write the letter on a separate sheet of paper.

1. a. Mrs. Meyer blows out her birthday candles. Then the firefighters cut the cake, and everyone at the party enjoys a piece. Afterward, A.J. and his friends return to Ella Mentry School.

    b. While Mrs. Meyer has her eyes closed, A.J. sneaks a taste of the frosting. But just then, Mrs. Meyer opens her eyes and catches him! In anger, she carries the cake off to the second floor of the firehouse and eats it all by herself.

c. The banner that says "Happy Birthday" slowly starts to slide down until it touches the candles on the cake. The candles light the banner on fire, and the fire spreads, even catching on Mrs. Meyer's pants! Finally, the firefighters use fire extinguishers to put the fire out.

Chapter 4:

Using Context Clues

English is a weird language. I suspect that's a big reason why so many kids have a hard time reading it. Very often, words and phrases mean something completely different from what you'd think. Or they're spelled completely different from the way they sound.

Take the word "through," as in "We went through the tunnel." That is a weird word. It sounds like it should have the letters *ew* in it. But that would be "threw," as in "she threw the ball." "Through" looks a lot like "thought" and "thorough" and "though,"

but it means something completely different from all those words.*

So I can hardly blame kids for not want-
ing to read. Reading is hard!

Luckily, there are strategies you can use
to make hard words easier to read and
understand. Most of the time, you can
sound a word out. Like, "ridiculous" may
look like a hard word. But break it up into
smaller pieces and sound it out—RI DIC U
LOUS. IN CRED I BLE. CALC U LATE. IM
POSS I BLE. Like that.

If you don't know the meaning of a word,
often you can figure it out from the words
around it. That's called using "context

*I'm getting confused just writing this!

clues." Look at this passage from *Ms. Hannah Is Bananas!* . . .

Ms. Hannah spun around so we could get the full effect of her new dress.

"It's beautiful!" Andrea said. She is always complimenting (that's a big word) grown-ups on everything.

Yes, "complimenting" is a big word. But you can figure out what it means because Andrea just told Ms. Hannah that her dress was beautiful. So "complimenting" probably means saying something nice about somebody.

I try to make My Weird School as easy as possible to read. There are no "hard" words. If I can't spell a word, I don't use it.

Sentences are short. There are no boring descriptions. One sentence flows into the next one. One paragraph flows into the next one.

 Another way to make stuff easy to read is to repeat it. Sentences are easier to read if you're not reading them for the first time. I say certain "catch phrases" over and over again in every My Weird School book. Here are some of them . . .

My name is A.J. and I hate _____.
That's the first rule of being a kid.
I thought I was gonna die.
Nah-nah-nah boo-boo!

That's when the weirdest thing in the history of the world happened.

He should get the Nobel Prize. That's a prize they give out to people who don't have bells.

Everybody laughed even though I didn't say anything funny.

"WOW!" everybody said, which is "MOM" upside down.

You'll never believe who walked into the door at that moment.

It was the greatest night of my life.

This was the worst thing to happen since TV Turnoff Week.

Andrea smiled the smile she smiles to let everybody know that she knows something nobody else knows.

Bummer in the summer!

Nobody knows why.

You should have *been* there!

We had to wait a million hundred hours.

What is her problem?

I didn't know what to say. I didn't know what to do. I had to think fast.

If those guys weren't my best friends, I would hate them.

We went back and forth like that for a while.

Run for your lives!

She never got the chance to finish her sentence because . . .

You can rent anything.

Sheesh! Get a grip!

There was electricity in the air.

We were on pins and needles.

We were all glued to our seats.

But it won't be easy!

 Reading tip from Andrea: What's your rush? Take your time. Enjoy the experience. Reading isn't a race.

Read this passage from *Mrs. Lane Is a Pain!*, in which A.J. delivers a stand-up comedy routine for the school talent show. Then use it to complete the activity that follows.

"Mr. Klutz is nuts!" I continued. "Remember the time he got his foot caught in a rope, and he got stuck at the top of the flagpole? You should have been there! We were all *glued to our seats*. Well, not really. That would be weird. Why would anybody glue himself to a seat? How would you get the glue off?"

Glue's Clues

An idiom (*id-i-om*) is a phrase that means something other than what the words suggest. For example, if your teacher says you're "in hot water," it means you're in trouble, and probably not that you're actually sitting in hot water. (That would be weird.) Often, the meaning of an idiom can be determined by **context clues**— other sentences and words in the text.

Directions: Look back at the passage from the talent show. Choose the correct definition for the italicized idiom based on the context clues.

We were all *glued to our seats* means
we were _____.

    a. In big trouble

    b. Paralyzed with fear

    c. Watching with great interest

    d. Doing arts and crafts

The Big Surprise Ending

Read this passage from *Mrs. Lane Is a Pain!*, in which A.J. and the other students wait to hear the results of the talent show. Notice the underlined idioms. Then use the passage to complete the activity that follows.

I hope I win. I hope I win. I hope I win. I hope I win. I hope I win.

"The winner is . . ."

Everybody got quiet as Mr. Porky tore open the envelope. *You could have heard a pin drop* in the all-purpose room.

Well, that is, if anybody had pins with them. But why would anybody bring pins to a talent show? That would be weird.

Anyway, *there was electricity in the air.*

Well, not really, because if there was electricity in the air, we all would have been electrocuted.

What I mean to say is, everybody in the audience was *on pins and needles*.

Well, not really. They were sitting on seats. It would have hurt if they were on pins and needles.

I bet you're *dying to know* who won the talent show, aren't you?

On Pins and Needles

Directions: In the space provided or on a separate piece of paper, select the correct meaning for each idiom. Remember to look for context clues from the passage!

1. *You could have heard a pin drop.*

   a. Hairpins were falling out of everyone's hair.

   b. The room was silent as people listened with interest.

   c. Everyone had super hearing.

   d. People were bored and distracted.

2. *There was electricity in the air.*

   a. People were excited.

   b. People were angry.

   c. People were taking cover from a storm.

   d. People were dancing.

3. *On pins and needles*

   a. Waiting with great anticipation

   b. Wincing with pain

   c. Running with quick feet

   d. Sewing a costume

4. *Dying to know*

   a. Interested in knowing

   b. Disappointed to learn

   c. Afraid to find out

   d. Mildly curious to hear

Homophones and Homographs

Homophones are words that sound the same when you read them out loud but have different spellings and meanings. For example, "to," "two," and "too" are homophones. **Homographs** are words that are spelled the same but have different meanings. They may or may not sound the same when you read them out loud. For example, there are sixty seconds in a "minute" (*mi-nut*), but something very small is "minute" (*my-noot*). Just as you can use context clues to figure out the definition of a big word or an idiom, you can use them to tell which version of a homophone or homograph you are reading.

Directions: Read the following sentence pairs featuring homophones, then use context clues to match the words with their correct definitions. Write the letter of the correct definition in the space provided or on a seperate sheet of paper.

1. Andrea is dressing up as a **witch** for Halloween! ____

2. **Which** Halloween candy is your favorite? ____

    a. Someone with magic powers who rides on a broom

    b. A word that specifies one or more things from a group

★ ★ ★

3. Bummer in the summer! It's the last **week** of vacation before school starts again! ____

4. During the Brain Games, the Dirk School's bridge was too **weak** to support the heavy barbell. ____

    a. Not able to sustain much weight or pressure

    b. A series of seven days

★ ★ ★

5. The sky was still **blue** when A.J. went up in Miss Newman's hot air balloon. ____

6. Then a storm came, and strong winds **blew** the balloon in every direction! ____

    a. A color

    b. The past tense of blow, a verb that means to move with air

Directions: Read the following sentences, then use context clues to choose the correct definition for the homographs in bold.

7. When Mr. Cooper gave his class a surprise math quiz, A.J. had to think hard to figure out the **right** answers.

   a. The opposite direction from left

   b. Correct

8. The movie about penguins was so sad, Andrea had a **tear** in her eye when it was over.

   a. A split or hole caused by something being ripped or torn

   b. A drop of fluid

9. Miss Daisy marked Alexia **present** when she called roll in the morning.

   a. A gift

   b. In attendance

Chapter 5:

Comparing and Contrasting

For me, one of the hardest things about reading a story is remembering all the characters. When there are a lot of characters in a book, I often get confused. Sometimes I take notes as I'm reading to help me remember who is who. You can try that too.

There are about sixty grown-ups in My Weird School, but each book focuses on just one, so you don't have to worry about keeping track of all sixty. There are seven kids. The boys are A.J., Ryan, Michael, and Neil.

 Yay!

The girls are Andrea, Emily, and Alexia.

 Boo!

Okay, calm down. A.J. and Andrea are the main characters. Except for the fact that they're both very smart, I made them total opposites so you'll never get them confused. A.J. is obnoxious, silly, immature, funny, and sometimes says mean things, especially to Andrea. Andrea is a smart, studious girl who loves to learn, is good at everything, and likes to impress grown-ups. A.J. says he hates everything. Andrea says she loves everything.

And oh, by the way, A.J. and Andrea are secretly in love with each other. I often tell kids that A.J. and Andrea will probably grow up and get married someday.

 Ugh! Gross! Disgusting! Pay no attention to him.

If A.J. and Andrea were very similar to each other, I think My Weird School would be boring. The books would also be harder to read, and maybe confusing. With these two main characters so *different* from each other, you can separate them in your head while you're reading. I bet some of you identify with one over the other, and silently root for A.J. or Andrea to be successful.

At some point, I thought it would be fun to give Andrea a rival for A.J.'s affections. That's when Alexia joined the class. She's a girl, but she is just like A.J. in every other way, right down to her initials.

 Alexia is cool.

I thought it would be fun to have one character that bad things happen to all the time. That's Emily, Andrea's emotional sidekick. She's always walking into walls, having things fall on her head, crying, and getting so scared that she runs out of the room.*

Ryan, Michael, and Neil are A.J.'s friends. I must confess they're not very different from one another. Like A.J., they say rude things and tease each other, maybe not as cleverly as A.J. I'll say one thing about boys, from my own experience. When we like each other, we make fun of each other.

Those are the My Weird School characters. I have no plans to add any other kids to the mix, because I'm afraid things would get confusing. But it *is* a little weird to have a class with only seven kids in it.

---

*To all the girls named Emily out there, I apologize.

Reading tip from Andrea: When you're reading, run your finger along the words as a guide as you read them. Sometimes I put a ruler or a piece of paper under the line I'm reading so I don't get distracted by the lines below that one.

Girls Rule. Boys Drool.

Characters in a story can be similar or different. They might be similar in some ways but different in others. Comparing and contrasting characters helps us to understand them better.

Read this passage from *Mayor Hubble Is in Trouble!*, in which A.J. and Andrea have a debate for the position of class president. Pay attention to whether A.J. and Andrea are similar, different, or both.

"And why do *you* want to be president, A.J.?" asked Mrs. Roopy.

"I want to be president so Andrea will not win," I admitted. "Because if she's president, we'll all be marching around in uniforms, doing extra homework, reading Shakespeare plays, taking dancing lessons, and singing songs from *Annie*."

"That's a lie!" Andrea protested.

"Let's move on," said Mrs. Roopy. "What do you think should be served for lunch at our cafetorium? Andrea?"

"I believe the students should have a healthy, nutritious meal every day," Andrea said. "And I will fight so that each and every one of us gets a balanced diet."

"That's right!" shouted Emily.

"I think we should be able to eat as much junk food as we want," I said.

"So, Andrea," said Mrs. Roopy, "would you ban junk food from the cafetorium?"

"Yes!" Andrea replied. "How will we grow up to be big and strong if we stuff ourselves with that poison?"

"There you go again," I said. "You want to take away our freedom, the freedom to poison ourselves. That's in the Bill of Rights, y'know."

"It is not!" Andrea shouted. "I memorized the Bill of Rights, and that's not one of them!"

"*My* Bill of Rights came with bonus features," I said. "Like a DVD."

Everybody laughed, even though I didn't say anything funny.

"Let's move on," said Mrs. Roopy. "Andrea, you have said that recess is too long, and that it takes time away from learning. But most kids say that recess is too short. What is your feeling now?"

"Well, I was for recess before I was against recess," Andrea said.

"Make up your mind!" I shouted at Andrea. "You're a flip-flopper!"

"I am not!" Andrea shouted. "You're mean, Arlo!"

"So is your face!" I replied.

"Well, you're not invited to my birthday party!" Andrea shouted at me.

Everybody gasped.

Mr. Venn Is an Alien

A **Venn diagram*** can be used to compare and contrast two or more ideas—or people. In a Venn diagram, circles are drawn to represent the things that are being compared. Traits that the things have in common are written into the space where the circles overlap, while traits that are different are written in the outside of the circles.

Directions: Read the following statements, which could describe A.J., Andrea, or both. Write them into the Venn diagram below (or make

*The Venn diagram was the idea of John Venn. Maybe someday you'll overlap two shapes and get a diagram named after you!

your own Venn diagram on a separate sheet of paper), showing whether you think they describe Andrea, A.J., or both.

Statements:

Wants to become class president

Is passionate about the debate

Is a quick thinker

Wants to ban junk food from the cafe-torium

Owns a copy of the Bill of Rights with bonus features

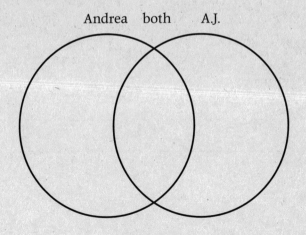

Andrea   both   A.J.

Team Andrea or Team A.J.?

Directions: In *Mayor Hubble Is in Trouble!*, Andrea says the perfect field trip would be to see the *Mona Lisa* in Paris, while A.J. says the perfect field trip would be to see Batman with free popcorn. Andrea believes every student should have a healthy, nutritious meal for lunch, while A.J. believes every student should get to eat as much junk food as they want.

Are you more like Andrea or A.J.? In the space below or on a separate piece of paper, fill in the blanks and then write three supporting sentences explaining why you made the choice you did.

My name is _____ and I am more like _____ than _____.

Because . . .

1. _____

_____

2. _____

_____

3. _____

_____

A Writing Lesson and the Big Surprise Ending

Read these two passages from *Miss Daisy Is Still Crazy!* and *Mr. Cooper Is Super!* Pay attention to how the two teachers are similar and how they are different.

Miss Daisy

"We're bored," said Neil. "Can you teach us about math or something?"

"Math?" asked Miss Daisy. "I hate math! Why do you need to know math? That's why we have calculators."

90

"But we want to learn something," said Andrea.

"Learning things is boring," said Miss Daisy. "Let's just talk. What do you want to talk about?"

"Can we talk about skateboards?" I suggested.

"Yeah," said Alexia. "Let's talk about skateboards."

"Great!" said Miss Daisy. "I love skateboarding. Hey, there's something I don't understand about skateboards. Maybe you kids can help me."

"Sure," I said. "I know everything there is to know about skateboards."

"I have these five friends," Miss Daisy

told me, "and I bought each of them a skateboard as a present. But the skateboards didn't come with wheels on them. So I have to buy wheels for all my friends. But I don't know how many wheels I need to buy. It's a big problem."

Hmmm, that was a tough one. I had to think about it.

Mr. Cooper

The next morning, Mr. Cooper came running into our classroom. He told us he was Lava Man, and he taught us all

about volcanoes. Then he ran out of the room and came back as Weather Man. He taught us all about meteorology. Then he ran out of the room and came back as Electric Man. He taught us all about electricity. It's fun to learn stuff from a superhero, whether he's a real superhero or not.

Weird in Opposite Ways

Directions: In the spaces below or on a separate sheet of paper, answer the questions in complete sentences.

1. In what weird way does Mr. Cooper teach the class about different science subjects, such as volcanoes, weather, and electricity?

_____

_____

_____

_____

2. What trick does Miss Daisy play to get her students to think about math?

_____

_____

_____

3. How are Mr. Cooper and Miss Daisy different in the way they teach kids?

_____

_____

_____

4. Can you think of a way that Mr. Cooper and Miss Daisy are similar?

_____

_____

_____

Make Your Own Teacher

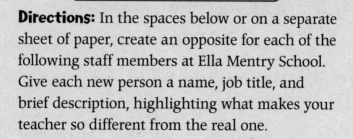

Directions: In the spaces below or on a separate sheet of paper, create an opposite for each of the following staff members at Ella Mentry School. Give each new person a name, job title, and brief description, highlighting what makes your teacher so different from the real one.

Example: Mr. Nick, the substitute principal, doesn't believe in rules.

Ms. Strict, the substitute vice principal, has rules about every little thing.

1. Ms. Leaky, the health teacher, is obsessed with exercise and healthy eating.

_____

_____

_____

2. Ms. Klute, the therapy dog, would rather play outside than be read to all day.

_____

_____

_____

3. Mrs. Lane, the talent show director, is quite talented herself!

_____

_____

_____

Reading tip from Andrea: You don't have to read boring books (unless you *have* to for school, of course!). Read what interests you. I like horses, so I look for books about them.

You like monster trucks? There are books about monster trucks. You like professional wrestling? There are books about professional wrestling. Whatever you're interested in, there are books about that subject. There are books about every subject in the world. And you know what? Once you start enjoying to read, you may find that those books that used to bore you aren't so boring anymore!

Chapter 6:

Sequencing and Cause & Effect

You may think My Weird School is just a bunch of silly jokes. Well, it *is* a bunch of silly jokes, but there's a method to the madness, as they say. Believe me, it takes a lot of work, thought, and careful planning to make these silly stories look effortless. I'll tell you how I do it.

 Borrrring! I'm outta here. See you in the next chapter.

There are around ten chapters in a My Weird School book, and each one is a little story by itself. The first chapter is very important, even though it usually doesn't have anything to do with the rest of the story. I'm just trying to grab you by the eyeballs in the first chapter and make you laugh.

I figure if I can hook you on the first page—or better yet, in the first *sentence*—you'll want to read Chapter 2. If you're not hooked in Chapter 1, you may just close the book and never pick it up again.

I do that all the time. Hundreds of thousands of books are published in the United States alone each year. I'm only going to read a tiny fraction of them. So I'm not going to waste my time on books that don't grab me in the first chapter. As they say, life is too short.

In the next few chapters, the main grown-up character of the book is introduced. She (in most of the books it's a she, but the male grown-ups are just as weird) will do some silly stuff to indicate that she's a little nutty.* In the middle of the story, the grown-up will start doing weirder stuff, and then the kids become increasingly concerned that she is crazy. Usually, there's a cafeteria (vomitorium) scene in which the kids eat lunch and discuss or argue over what to do about the situation.

Then we build toward the ending. There's going to be some kind of event

_____

*But not *too* nutty, because she's got to get nuttier as the story goes on.

that can go horribly wrong. The graduation ceremony in *Mrs. Dole Is Out of Control!* The cell phone duel in *Mr. Burke Is Berserk!* The birthday cake scene in *Mrs. Meyer Is on Fire!* So one event causes the next event, and the next one, and the next one.

And finally, at the end, things usually spin out of control and everything gets crazy, with everyone running around like lunatics. Each book ends with a bunch of ridiculous sentences that start with the word "maybe." The last sentence is always, "But it won't be easy!"

So that's a very general outline for a My Weird School book. In most books, the author is trying to take you on a journey like that. When you know how a story is going to flow, it makes it easier to read. But of course, authors also want to surprise and amaze you, so we try to be unpredictable. As you read a story, notice the familiar patterns as well as the unexpected things the author put in to keep you interested.

 Reading tip from Andrea: You like comic books or graphic novels? There's nothing wrong with that. You can read song lyrics, websites, blogs, or restaurant place mats. Read the back of your cereal box!

Okay, So I Lied

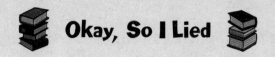

Read the passage from *Miss Newman Isn't Human!*, in which A.J., Andrea, and meteorologist Miss Newman ride a hot air balloon through a haboob (a type of dust storm).

Okay, so I lied. I told you there was no such thing as a haboob, and there would be no more haboobs in this book. And guess what? It turns out "haboob" is a real word, and it's part of the story!

"Cover your faces!" yelled Miss Newman. "Keep the sand out of your eyes and nose!"

She didn't have to tell me. I pulled my T-shirt over my face to keep the sand away.

"What are we going to do?" shouted Andrea.

"There's nothing to do but ride it out!" Miss Newman yelled back. "The haboob could be moving forty miles an hour."

Wow! That might be fast enough to blow the school away. And if the school blows away, there will be no school! Yay!

But right now I had other things to worry about. The basket was swaying back and forth. I was afraid the whole thing might flip over.

"Are we going to die?" I shouted.

"Not on my watch," Miss Newman shouted back.

What did watches have to do with

anything? She wasn't even wearing a watch.

Miss Newman grabbed some ropes on the side of the basket and pulled on them. I guess it was for steering or something. The basket stopped swaying.

"This is a dangerous situation," she hollered over the sound of the wind and sand blowing in our faces. "I need to report the weather to the people!"

"How are you going to do that?" Andrea shouted.

"Grab that camera off the floor," Miss Newman yelled. "We have a satellite linkup so we can transmit the signal back to Channel 4."

"I have sand in my eyes!" Andrea hollered. "I can't see!"

"I got it," I yelled as I picked up the camera. "What do you want me to do?"

"Push the red button and point the camera at me," Miss Newman yelled back.

I did what she said.

"This is Sprinkles Newman, of Channel 4 weather," she hollered. "I'm coming to you live from the middle of a haboob. That's an intense sandstorm. If you're outside, I need you to get inside right away. If you can't get inside, cover your nose and mouth with cloth."

The camera was heavy. But I kept pointing it at Miss Newman.

"If you're in your car driving somewhere, pull over right away," she shouted. "Almost every death caused by a haboob has been because people try to drive cars through them and they crash into things."

She went on like that for a while, talking about which direction the haboob was heading and how fast it was moving. She sure knows a lot about haboobs!

Finally, the haboob blew past us. The sky got calm. Miss Newman steered the balloon so we were coming down in a field across the street from where we took off. The whole school came running over.

Well, not really. Schools can't run.

They don't have legs. But all the kids

and teachers came running over. They were cheering and clapping.

"We saw you on TV!" everybody shouted.

"That was cool, A.J.," said Neil. "You're famous!"

This was the greatest day of my life. Mr. Klutz helped us climb out of the basket. All the teachers were taking pictures with their cell phones.

"Arlo, you were sooooo brave filming that video!" said Andrea.

And then she did the most horrible thing in the history of the world. She kissed me.

Ugh, gross! This was the worst day of my life!

"Ooooo!" Ryan said. "Andrea kissed A.J. and said he was brave. They must be in *love*!"

"When are you gonna get married?" asked Michael.

Breaking News

In a story, the **sequence of events** is the order in which things happen, from the beginning to the middle to the end.

Directions: In the spaces below or on a separate sheet of paper, put the sequence of events in the correct order using the details from the story. The first event in the sequence has been done for you.

  a. The haboob blows over, and the sky grows calm.

  b. Andrea kisses A.J.

  c. Miss Newman warns her viewers to get inside right away.

  d. A.J. uses his T-shirt to cover his face from the sand.

e. Miss Newman lands the balloon in a field.

f. A.J. picks up the camera and starts recording Miss Newman.

1. <u>d</u>
2. ____
3. ____
4. ____
5. ____
6. ____

What to Do in a Haboob

When something makes another thing happen, the first thing is called a **cause** and the second thing is called an **effect**. For example, if you run into a door, it would really hurt, and you might even cry. In that case, running into the door would be the cause, and crying would be the effect.

Directions: In the space below or on a separate sheet of paper, draw a line from the cause to the effect.

Cause	Effect
"Cover your faces!" yelled Miss Newman.	"I got it," I yelled as I picked up the camera.
Finally, the haboob blew past us.	I pulled my T-shirt over my face to keep the sand away.
"Grab the camera off the floor," Miss Newman yelled.	The sky got calm.
She kissed me!	"When are you gonna get married?" asked Michael.

Chapter 7:

Facts, Opinions, Inferences,

and Hyperboles

★ ★ ★

There's nothing funny about a banana that weighs a pound. If I write that a banana weighs ten *thousand* pounds, it's funny because it's so obviously not true. You picture a ten-thousand-pound banana in your head. But if I say an elephant weighs ten thousand pounds, it's not funny, because some elephants really *do* weigh ten thousand pounds.*

---

*A one-pound elephant? Now *that* would be funny.

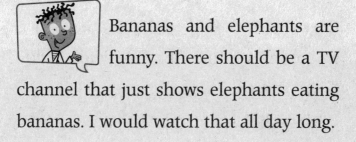Bananas and elephants are funny. There should be a TV channel that just shows elephants eating bananas. I would watch that all day long.

It's probably on YouTube. The point is, when you expect one thing and you read something completely different, it can be funny. School is supposed to be a *serious* place with *serious* grown-ups helping kids learn *serious* things. So it's funny when these grown-ups do silly things instead. Mr. Klutz, the principal, hangs upside down from a pole in his office. Mrs. Roopy, the librarian, pretends to be Johnny Appleseed. Dr. Carbles, the president of the Board of Education, drives a tank down the street. Mrs. Leakey, the health teacher, is caught stuffing her face with candy bars.

The whole point of My Weird School is to exaggerate the real world until it becomes ridiculous and (hopefully) funny. Art teachers like Ms. Hannah like to collect stuff for projects, but they don't ask the garbagemen to deliver garbage to the school. Coaches like Coach Hyatt make their players work hard, but they don't have them pick up cars. Computer teachers like Mrs. Yonkers know a lot about technology, but they don't invent machines that turn vegetables into junk food. Sometimes I don't even *have* to exaggerate the real world. In the My Weird School Fast Facts series, I simply collect the weirdest, funniest facts, organize them, and have A.J. and Andrea argue about them.

While you're reading, notice the facts, fictions, and exaggerations (also called hyperboles). When A.J. says he has to walk a million hundred miles, you know he's just saying it's a long walk. When he says he wishes he could run away to Antarctica and live with the penguins, you know he's just frustrated. Sometimes the truth, lies, and exaggerations aren't so obvious. It's important to be able to spot the difference.

Could Dinosaurs Swim?

Read this passage from the nonfiction book *My Weird School Fast Facts: Dinosaurs, Dodos, and Woolly Mammoths,* then use it to complete the activities that follow.

 Back in prehistoric times, there were pictures of huge dinosaurs like *Apatosaurus* and *Diplodocus* swimming in swamps and lakes. In those days, scientists believed their bodies were so big that their legs couldn't support their weight on land.

 The scientists were so big that their legs couldn't support their weight on land?

Not the scientists, Arlo! The dinosaurs!

 Oh. Why didn't you say so?

 Anyway, the theory was wrong. A scientist named K. A. Kermack found that water pressure would have crushed the thorax of an underwater dinosaur and cut off its air supply.

 Ouch! That's gotta hurt.

 Most dinosaurs were land animals. When they find a

dinosaur skeleton at the bottom of a lake, that doesn't mean the dinosaur lived or died there. It could have been moved there by a predator or a landslide. But most land animals can swim at least a little if they fall into water, so some dinosaurs probably could too.

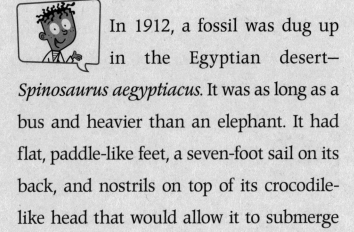 In 1912, a fossil was dug up in the Egyptian desert—*Spinosaurus aegyptiacus.* It was as long as a bus and heavier than an elephant. It had flat, paddle-like feet, a seven-foot sail on its back, and nostrils on top of its crocodile-like head that would allow it to submerge underwater. Scientists believe Spinosaurus

is the first-known dinosaur adapted for swimming.

 So I guess the answer is yes, some dinosaurs could swim. But it's not like they would be able to pass a lifesaving test or anything.

 I have a question. Could dinosaurs play musical instruments?

 No! Why would you even ask a silly question like that? That doesn't make any sense at all!

Well, some dinosaurs can fly, right? And it seems to me that it's a lot easier to play a musical instrument than it is to fly. My sister, Amy, can play the piano really well, but she can't fly at all. So it makes perfect sense for dinosaurs to play musical instruments. I think it would be cool to see a dinosaur play a tuba.

Jurassic Facts and Dino-pinions

A **fact** is a statement that has been proven to be true. An **opinion** is a belief that cannot be proven true or false because it is personal to an individual or to a group. An **inference** is an educated guess based on outside knowledge. Like predictions, inferences are strongest when they are based on evidence.

Directions: In the spaces provided or on a separate sheet of paper, write **F** if the statement is a fact, **O** if it is an opinion, or **I** if it is an inference.

Most land animals can swim at least a little if they fall into water, so some dinosaurs probably could too. _____(1)

When they find a dinosaur skeleton at the bottom of a lake, it could have been moved there by a predator or a landslide. _____(2)

In 1912, a fossil was dug up in the Egyptian desert–*Spinosaurus aegyptiacus*. _____(3)

I think it would be cool to see a dinosaur play a tuba. _____(4)

Shopping Is Way Overrated

A **hyperbole** is a figure of speech that uses exaggeration for emphasis or humor. For example, did you ever say you were *starving* when you were just a little hungry? That's a hyperbole.

Read this passage from *Ms. Leakey Is Freaky!*, told from A.J.'s point of view, then use it to complete the activity that follows.

Shopping is way overrated. I don't know if you ever went grocery shopping with your mom or dad, but it is the most boring thing in the history of the world. We had to go up and down every aisle of the supermarket. I thought I was gonna die. All I wanted was my treat.

When my mom buys a melon, she acts like she's buying a house. She has to feel each melon. She has to smell each melon. Then she has to shake each melon and listen to it. What is her problem?

"It's just a *melon*!" I said. "They're all the same."

"I have to find the *perfect* melon," she said.

I hate melon.

Finally, after a million hundred hours, she found the perfect melon. We were finished grocery shopping.

"So, what treat do you want, A.J.?" my mom asked.

I had been thinking about it the whole time we were shopping. At first I wanted an ice cream-pop. But I decided that an ice-cream pop wouldn't last very long. Then I wanted a Devil Dog. But they come in boxes of eight, and I knew my mom would say I could only get *one* treat.

Then I saw something at the end of the candy aisle. It was a giant box filled to the brim with candy. Just about every kind of candy in the world was in there. I led my mom over to it.

"Okay, you can have *one* treat, A.J.," my mom said. "Just one. I'll get in line. You choose your treat and meet me in the checkout line."

I looked over the candy: Milky Way,

AirHeads, Mars bars, Twix, Kit Kat, Chunky, Mr. Goodbar, York Peppermint Patties, Reese's Peanut Butter Cups, Mike and Ike, Atomic FireBall, JuJu Fish, Sour Neon Worms, Goobers, Laffy Taffy, Nerds, Sugar Daddy, Baby Ruth, Snickers, Kisses, M&M's (plain *and* peanut), gummi bears, Dots, Junior Mints, Milk Duds, Good & Plenty, Whoppers, Twizzlers, Dum Dums, Skittles, Butterfinger, Starburst, Crunch, Jolly Rancher, Sweet Pops, Tootsie Roll. . . .

I couldn't decide which one I wanted. Everything looked so good. I wanted them *all*. I thought and thought and thought until my brain was about to explode. Finally, I decided to get a 3 Musketeers bar.

I leaned all the way over.

I reached out to pick up the 3 Muske-teers bar.

I picked up the 3 Musketeers bar.

And you'll never believe in a million hundred years what happened next.

A Million Hundred Hyperboles

Directions: In the space below or on a separate sheet of paper, list all the hyperboles you found in the text.

_____

_____

_____

_____

Bonus: Make a list of hyperboles you use in your everyday life.

_____

_____

_____

_____

Chapter 8:

Expanded Sentences

Some sentences are long, and some sentences are short. That's a good thing. If all sentences were the same length, they would be boring. Just like it would be boring to ride a roller coaster if it didn't go up and down.

 That's called riding in a car.

Right! Really long sentences are harder to read. In my writing, I usually try to break long sentences down into shorter ones to make them easier for you to read. Like this!

Sometimes kids will write very long sentences with lots of adjectives and adverbs because they've been told that writing should be descriptive. Me, I'm the opposite. I say get rid of those adjectives and adverbs unless you really need them.

There's no reason to write the phrase "blue sky," because everybody knows the sky is blue. And usually, there's no reason to write "blue shirt" either. Not all shirts are blue, but the color of somebody's shirt probably doesn't matter to the story. So why put it in? To fill up lots of pages? A story that has lots of pages isn't necessarily a good story.

When I was a kid, I remember being

forced to read long, boring books that went on for page after page after page describing a character's shirt, or their face, or a room, or (worst of all) the weather.* That was one reason why I didn't like to read when I was a kid. I say get on with the story. Get to the point.

Having said that, every so often I like to use a long sentence instead of a short one. Like when A.J. says, "Everybody was yelling and screaming and hooting and hollering and freaking out!"

I could have simply written "Everybody was going crazy!" But I think the longer version tells you (the reader) that everything was *really* crazy.

---

*What a snoozefest!

Another example: In *Miss Child Has Gone Wild!*, A.J. says, "Her hair fell all the way down her back and swirled in slow motion, just like in those shampoo commercials on TV." I could have simply written "She had long hair." But the longer sentence (hopefully) puts a more powerful image in your head.

I guess what I'm trying to say is that it's easier to read a sentence that's short, simple, and to the point. But sometimes a long sentence can help make a story come alive.

 Reading tip from Andrea: Some kids don't like to sit still. Try reading while you're walking around a track, or on a treadmill.

Can You Expand on That?

A **complete sentence** needs only a **subject** and a **predicate**. The predicate is the part of the sentence that contains the verb. An **expanded sentence** includes extra words and phrases, like adjectives, adverbs, and prepositional phrases, to modify the subject or verb. Another way to expand a sentence is to combine two or more shorter sentences with **conjunctions** like "and" or "but."

Directions: In the spaces below or on a separate sheet of paper, join these sentences from *Mr. Nick Is a Lunatic!* with one of the conjunctions from the box. You may use a conjunction more than once.

My name is A.J. _____(1) I hate when an asteroid crashes into the earth and wipes out all life on our planet.

We thought that was the end of it, ____(2) you'll never believe who came running through the door at that moment.

The top of the tank opened up, _____(3) you'll never believe in a million hundred years whose head popped out.

There was no point in shaking our butts at the class, _____(4) we already did that.

It was one o'clock in the afternoon, _____(5) maybe it was two o'clock.

A bunch of firefighters jumped off the fire truck with hoses, _____(6) they started spraying water at Mr. Klutz and our teachers.

Compound Subjects
and Predicates

When two or more sentences share the same subject, you can combine them to form one longer sentence with a **compound predicate**, using commas and conjunctions like "and" or "but."

For example, these sentences have the same subject:

a. A.J. went to the front of the class.

b. A.J. performed his stand-up comedy.

c. A.J. received a round of applause from the class.

As a result, you can combine them into one sentence with a compound predicate:

A.J. went to the front of the class, performed his stand-up comedy, **and** received a round of applause from the class.

Directions: Combine each of the following groups of sentences into one sentence with a compound predicate, using "and" or "but."

1. a. Mr. Cooper pulled out his math textbook.

   b. Mr. Cooper told the class to turn to page twenty-three.

   _____

   _____

   _____

   _____

   _____

2. a. Emily turned around.

   b. Emily leaned in.

   c. Emily whispered a secret to Andrea.

   _____

   _____

_____

_____

_____

_____

3. a. Alexia took the class pet home.

   b. Alexia forgot to feed him.

_____

_____

_____

_____

_____

When two or more sentences share the same predicate, you can combine them to form one longer sentence with a **compound subject**, using commas and conjunctions like "and" or "or."

For example, these sentences have the same predicate:

a. A.J. went to the grocery store.

b. Ryan went to the grocery store.

c. Neil went to the grocery store.

As a result, you can combine them into one sentence with a compound subject:

A.J., Ryan, and Neil went to the grocery store.

Directions: Combine each of the following groups of sentences into one sentence with a compound subject, using "and" or "or."

4. a. The students are ready for summer vacation.

   b. The teachers are ready for summer vacation.

   _____

   _____

   _____

   _____

5. a. Andrea wanted to see the *Mona Lisa* in Paris.

   b. Alexia wanted to see the *Mona Lisa* in Paris.

   c. Pierre wanted to see the *Mona Lisa* in Paris.

_____

_____

_____

_____

6. a. Ryan can take the library book home tonight.

   b. Neil can take the library book home tonight.

_____

_____

_____

_____

Alphabet Soup

Directions: A.J. ate some weird alphabet soup in the vomitorium. Now every time he talks, his sentences keep expanding with more words! Starting with these two simple sentences, add the conjunctions and modifiers listed below and see how long you can make your final sentence! Use the spaces provided or a separate sheet of paper.

Simple sentences:

    a. My name is A.J.

    b. I hate rain.

1. Now combine these two sentences into one sentence using a conjunction:

_____

_____

_____

2. Now add an **adjective** or two to your sentence. An adjective is a word that describes a noun. For example, instead of just "rain," you might write "loud rain" or "unexpected purple rain."

_____

_____

_____

3. Now add an **adverb** or two to your sentence. An adverb is a word that describes a verb and often ends in "-ly." For example, instead of just "hate," you might write "seriously hate" or "truly, madly, deeply hate."

_____

_____

_____

_____

_____

4. Now add a **prepositional phrase** to the end your sentence. A prepositional phrase is a phrase that begins with a preposition like "into," "at," or "on" and ends with an object, usually a noun or a pronoun. For example, instead of just "My name is A.J., and I seriously hate loud rain," you might write "My name is A.J., and I seriously hate loud rain on the playground."

_____

_____

_____

_____

_____

Now *that's* an expanded sentence!

Simplify, Simplify, Simplify

Directions: Now try it in reverse! In the space below or on a separate piece of paper, delete the adjectives, adverbs, and prepositional phrases, then rewrite the simplified sentences for A.J.

 1. My name is A.J. and I strongly, vehemently, passionately hate green, sticky, slimy snot.

_____

_____

 2. Ms. Kraft quickly ran into the brown wooden door at that moment.

_____

_____

3. Mr. Cooper proudly, deliberately wears a short red cape.

_____

_____

Reading tip from Andrea: Read your regular book along with the audio book version of it. This helps you pronounce some of the words, and shows you what to do when you come to commas, periods, question marks, and exclamation points.

Chapter 9:

Point of View and Characters

When my daughter, Emma, was in second grade, she liked reading Junie B. Jones books. We both thought that it would be interesting if there was something *like* Junie B. Jones told by a boy. That's what inspired the first My Weird School book, *Miss Daisy Is Crazy!**

Every story is told from a "point of view." It might be one of the characters, or it might be the author. I didn't think My Weird School should be told from *my*

---

*You may have noticed that most of the books in the series are dedicated "To Emma."

point of view, because you kids wouldn't relate to a middle-aged guy who went to elementary school fifty years ago. But I *remember* what it was like to be a kid in elementary school, and I also visit about forty schools a year to remind me what kids are like. So I invented this fictional character named A.J. to tell the story of My Weird School from *his* point of view. (*Back to School, Weird Kids Rule!* is from Andrea's point of view.)

 Wait a minute. I'm *fictional*? You mean I don't exist in the real world?

That's right. You're based on real kids, but you're not real.

 Yippee! If I'm not real, that means I don't have to go to school anymore!

As I mentioned in Chapter 5, A.J. is a silly, funny, and often obnoxious little boy. Sometimes people send me emails complaining that the language or content of My Weird School is inappropriate (or worse) for kids. I try to explain to them that A.J. is a pretty typical boy, and that's the way boys sometimes talk. If A.J. was nice to everybody all the time, he wouldn't seem real. I hope that kids will laugh at A.J.'s silly words and not take them too seriously.

As My Weird School goes on, I see A.J. growing up just a little bit, becoming more mature. In *Bummer in the Summer!*, he sees the effect his past words and actions have had on other people, and it changes his point of view. It may make him a little nicer.

 Never! You can't make me! So nah-nah-nah boo-boo on you!

Reading tip from Andrea: If you don't understand a word or phrase, ask for help. Or look it up in a dictionary.

Talent Show Mix-Up and Teamwork Trouble

Point of view refers to the perspective from which a story is told. When a story is told using **first-person point of view**, the narrator is a character in the story and uses statements that include "I" and "my." Most of the My Weird School books are told from A.J.'s first-person point of view, but some are told from the point of view of other characters. When a story is told using **third-person point of view**, the narrator is not a character in the story, but the narrator might know the characters' thoughts (third-person omniscient) or might not (third-person limited).

Read the passages from *Talent Show Mix-Up* and *Teamwork Trouble*, which are told from A.J.'s and Ryan's points of view.

A.J.'s Point of View

My name is A.J. and I hate school. Monday was the worst. First my teacher, Mr. Cooper, passed out some papers.

"Exam time!" he said.

"Exam?" I said. "I just went to the doctor!"

Everyone laughed, even though I didn't say anything funny.

"He means the *test* kind of exam," said know-it-all Andrea. "Not the doctor kind. Duh!"

So we took a dumb math test.

Then Mr. Cooper said, "Tomorrow will be much more fun. It's our class talent show!"

Talent show? Ugh. I'd rather have an exam. The test kind OR the doctor kind!

At recess, Andrea acted all worried.

"I have too many talents," she said. "Should I sing at the show? Or dance? Or play the flute?"

"How about you sing solo," I said. "*So low* we can't hear you!"

Ryan's Point of View

My name is Ryan and I love sports. Baseball. Dodgeball. Basketball. Anything with a ball.

I play on a football team with A.J. and Andrea. They argue about *everything*. If Andrea says blue Sportzgulp is better, A.J. says red.

"Quit yelling," I told A.J. at our last game. "I'm trying to ask you something. Do you want to play on another team with me?"

"What sport?" asked A.J. "Soccer?"

"Um, no," I said. "Curling."

A.J. started laughing. He spit red Sportz-gulp everywhere.

"*Curling?* Isn't that what girls do to their hair?"

"It's a real sport," I said. "It's in the Olympics."

"Big deal!" said A.J. "So is trampoline, and everyone knows that's just bouncing."

"Fine," I said. "Hey Andrea. Want to be on a curling team?"

"Yes! I LOVE curling!" said Andrea. "I take lessons every week."

"See?" A.J. said. "It *must* be lame!"

Ryan Gets His Say

Directions: In the spaces below or on a separate sheet of paper, answer the multiple-choice questions about the two passages.

1. Why does Ryan mention that if Andrea says blue Sportzgulp is better, then A.J. says red? _____

    a. To explain to readers what flavors of Sportzgulp are available.

    b. To persuade readers that red Sportzgulp is better than blue.

    c. To give readers an example of how he sees A.J. and Andrea arguing.

    d. To convince readers that Andrea is right, while A.J. is wrong.

2. How does Ryan's point of view differ
from A.J.'s? _____

    a. A.J. thinks that Andrea is great,
but Ryan thinks she is a know-it-
all.

    b. A.J. thinks Andrea is the
annoying one, but Ryan thinks
A.J. and Andrea are both
annoying because of their
arguing.

    c. Ryan thinks that A.J. and Andrea
are perfect, but A.J. thinks he and
Andrea are not perfect.

    d. Ryan likes Andrea better than
A.J., but A.J. likes himself better
than Andrea.

3. What is A.J.'s point of view toward the talent show? _____

    a. A.J. is excited for the talent show.

    b. A.J. doesn't care one way or the other about the talent show.

    c. A.J. would rather take a test than participate in the talent show.

    d. A.J. is excited to watch Andrea perform in the talent show.

4. What is Ryan's point of view toward sports? _____

    a. He loves playing sports but gets annoyed when his friends make mistakes.

    b. He loves playing sports but only if he is the best.

    c. He loves playing only the sports

he already knows how to play,
like soccer and football.

d. He loves playing all sports,
including new ones.

5. Based on the passages, what are A.J.'s
and Ryan's points of view about trying
new things? _____

a. Ryan feels nervous about trying
new things, and A.J. loves trying
new things.

b. A.J. feels nervous about trying new
things, and Ryan loves trying new
things.

c. Ryan and A.J. both love trying
new things.

d. Both A.J. and Ryan feel nervous
about trying new things.

My Weird School Goes to the Museum

Read the passage from *My Weird School Goes to the Museum*, noticing how Andrea's point of view is different from A.J.'s.

My name is Andrea and I LOVE school! I love tests! I love homework! I love teachers—and teachers love ME!

"Teacher's pet!" A.J. calls me.

He thinks it's an insult, but I love it.

Who *wouldn't* want to be the teacher's favorite? A.J., that's who. All he wants to be is class clown.

He doesn't even care that he's in gifted and talented. I LOVE being in gifted and

talented! We're the only ones in the class. So we get to go on field trips, just the two of us.

"Ooooh," Ryan said this morning. "A.J. and Andrea are going to the art museum together. They must be in love!"

Well, duh. Of course we are. A.J. just doesn't know it yet.

"When are you two getting married?" said Michael.

"NEVER!" yelled A.J.

Ha. That's what he thinks.

"Remember to behave at the museum," warned Mr. Cooper.

He looked at A.J. when he said it. Teachers never look at me when they give warnings.

Everybody Loves Andrea

Directions: It's plain to see that Andrea is A.J.'s opposite. In the space below or on a separate sheet of paper, rewrite Andrea's passage from A.J.'s point of view. As a hint, we've started the passage for you.

My name is A.J. and I hate school.

_____

_____

_____

_____

_____

_____

_____

_____

Reading tip from Andrea: When you see a word you don't understand, stretch it out, like a rubber band. Sound out each letter. If a character in a story has a really long name that's hard to sound out (like Rumpel-stiltskin), just use the first initial (R!).

Chapter 10:

"Reading" Illustrations

Babies can't read words, so their books are pretty much just filled with pictures. Fifth and sixth graders usually read very well, so their books have few pictures. Kids *your* age are in various stages of mastering reading, so books for you have some pictures sprinkled around the pages.

A My Weird School book wouldn't be the same without words, and it also wouldn't be the same without pictures. It's the words and pictures *together* that tell the story.

Just like we can read words, we can also "read" pictures. You may not even realize it, but looking at the pictures gives you clues about the words you'll be reading. The pictures help you imagine in your mind what's going on in the story, and they make reading easier and more fun.

For example, in *Mr. Sunny Is Funny!*, A.J. has been told to watch out for sand monsters at the beach. There's no such thing as a sand monster. Nobody knows what a sand monster looks like. So on page ten, there's a picture of one. The drawing shows what A.J. is *imagining*. So you can "see" what's going on in his head.

Before you crack open a book, look at the covers and flip through the pages to look at the pictures. That will make the story more fun and easier to read.

I can't draw. The pictures in My Weird School are drawn by illustrator Jim Paillot. Lots of kids (and grown-ups) are surprised to hear that Jim and I have created more than sixty books together, but we've only met *once* in person. I live in New York City, and Jim lives over two thousand miles away, in Arizona. It would be pretty hard for us to meet for lunch and work on My Weird School.

So here's how we do it . . .

1. I write a short summary of the story (let's say, *Mr. Will Needs to Chill!*) and email it to my editor, Andrew. Mr. Will is an ice cream man.

2. Andrew emails it to Jim, who starts working on the cover. He doesn't know much more than that the story will be about an ice cream man. So he brainstorms and researches pictures of ice cream men.

3. While he's drawing the cover, I write the story (it takes about a month) and email it to Andrew.

4. Andrew emails my manuscript to Jim, who reads it and looks for scenes that would make good illustrations.

5. Jim draws those pictures (on his computer, by the way) and emails them to the art director at HarperCollins, the publishing company.

6. The art director designs the pages

with all the text, pictures, footnotes, page numbers, and chapter titles.

7. We all look over the finished pages carefully to make sure there are no mistakes.

8. The book is printed on some big printing press in Wisconsin.*

 Reading tip from Andrea: Try reading to yourself, silently. Sometimes reading out loud can actually slow you down. Your brain is faster than your mouth. Then try reading out loud— to your dog! Or your cat. Or a stuffed animal. They won't judge you.

---

*9. You read it!

A Picture Is Worth a Million Hundred Words

Illustrations help to tell a story. For instance, the expressions on the characters' faces can show how they are feeling.

Directions: Study this illustration from *Mr. Nick Is a Lunatic!* Then circle the emotion that best describes how each character is feeling, or write it on a separate sheet of paper.

1. Andrea: **Happy Sad Angry**
2. Ryan: **Happy Sad Angry**
3. Michael: **Happy Sad Angry**

Bonus: Based on the details in this picture, what do you think is happening in this scene?

_____

_____

_____

_____

_____

A Big Check

Directions: Study this illustration from *Ms. Cuddy Is Nutty!* Then answer the questions in the space below or on a separate sheet of paper.

1. Look at the check in the picture. Who signed the check?

_____

2. Who do you think Ella Mentry School is named after?

_____

3. Who is the woman in the picture?

_____

4. What is happening in this picture?

_____

The Truth About Mrs. Meyer

Read this passage from *Mrs. Meyer Is on Fire!*, told from A.J.'s point of view. Picture the details described. Then use the passage to complete the activity that follows.

We were eating lunch in the vomitorium. I had a peanut butter and jelly sandwich. Michael had a peanut butter and jelly sandwich. Ryan had a peanut butter and jelly sandwich. *Everybody* had peanut butter and jelly sandwiches. I traded my peanut butter and jelly sandwich for Neil's peanut butter and jelly sandwich because his mom cuts the crusts off.

"You know what's weird?" I told the gang. "Sometimes they say that a house burned down. And sometimes they say that a house burned up. But it's the same thing!"

"That's right," said Ryan. "Whether your house burns up or down, you still have no house left."

"I'll tell you what's weird," said Michael. "Mrs. Meyer."

"Yeah!" we all agreed.

"She's always telling jokes about fire," said Alexia.

"Hey, I know a fire joke," I said. "What do you call a doll that's on fire?"

"What?" everybody asked.

"A Barbie-Q."

Everybody laughed. Neil the nude kid laughed so hard that milk came out of his nose. You know a joke is good if you can make milk come out of somebody's nose. That's the first rule of being a kid.

A Scene from the Vomitorium

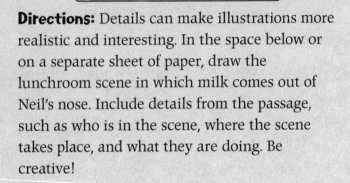

Directions: Details can make illustrations more realistic and interesting. In the space below or on a separate sheet of paper, draw the lunchroom scene in which milk comes out of Neil's nose. Include details from the passage, such as who is in the scene, where the scene takes place, and what they are doing. Be creative!

Chapter II:

Poetry and Rhymes

I grew up reading books by Dr. Seuss, and having my parents read them to me. In fact, the only books I remember really enjoying as a child were Dr. Seuss books. He used a lot of rhyming in his stories, and that's probably why I use a lot of rhyming in My Weird School.

As much as A.J. says he hates everything to do with school, he is such a natural rhyme machine that the gifted and talented teacher, Ms. Coco, thinks he's a genius. Mr. Hynde, the music teacher, is a rapper who frequently shows up spitting rhymes. And of course, the titles of the My

Weird School books themselves all rhyme. I've had fun coming up with titles featuring words that rhyme but are spelled differently, like Hynde/Mind, Louie/Screwy, Granite/Planet, Hyatt/Riot . . .

 Okay, we *get* it. Blah blah blah blah.*

Why do people like rhymes so much? There's something fun about words that rhyme. They make a pleasing ring in your brain when you say them or hear them.

I think rhymes also help make reading easier, because you know how a word is

*. . . Burke/Berserk, Beard/Weird, Hubble/Trouble, Klute/Hoot, Cooper/Super, Meyer/Fire, Newman/Human, Porter/Order . . .

going to sound before you get to it in the sentence.

If I write a rap or a poem with the line "Don't be a weenie. Just eat a _____," you know the last word is going to end with the sound "eenie." And you know it's going to be a food because of the word "eat." Not many foods end with the sound "eenie." But even a kid who doesn't know how to read yet will probably be able to predict that the last word of the line is going to be "zucchini."

 What's a zucchini? Is that some green thing? I don't eat stuff that's green.

Reading tip from Andrea: Try this trick. Start reading a line on the third word instead of the first word. Your brain is really smart, and it's going to "see" the first two words even if you're not trying to read them.

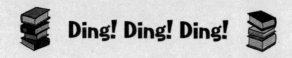

Ding! Ding! Ding!

Songs and poems are similar in that both have **rhythm** and often **rhyme**. In poetry, rhythm refers to the beat of the language, made using the syllables of the words. Rhyme refers to words that have the same sounds.

In *Mrs. Master Is a Disaster!*, the students invent a high-tech toilet seat called the Party Pooper. Read the rap that former music teacher Mr. Hynde writes to help them sell the seat.

How can you pee when you cannot see?

That's what folks keep asking me.

Pooping gets old

when your seat's too cold.

At least that's what I have been told.

You want it heated while you are seated.

You want it hot when you're on the pot.

You want it lit up while you sit up.

You want that glow when you gotta go.

That's why you need Party Pooper.

I said, Party Pooper! Party Pooper!

The Party Pooper is super-duper,

like Mrs. Master and Mr. Cooper.

This toilet seat is very fine,

and it only costs $99.99.

The best part about this toilet is
you'll never have to oil it, kids.
So get rid of your seat.
It can't compete
with the coolest toilet
out on the street.
And it smells so sweet.
Send out a tweet.
You'll get a receipt.
Let me repeat.
It's really neat.
The hottest seat
out on the street
is Party Pooper. . . .

Party Pooper Poetry

A **stanza** is a group of lines in a poem. Stanzas are usually separated by a blank line. Often, the lines in a stanza follow a **rhyme scheme**, such as AABB, in which lines one and two rhyme, and lines three and four rhyme; ABAB, in which lines one and three rhyme, and lines two and four rhyme; or ABBA, in which lines one and four rhyme, and lines two and three rhyme. The "A" lines rhyme with each other, and the "B" lines rhyme with each other.

Directions: In the space below or on a separate sheet of paper, answer the following questions about the Party Pooper rap.

1. How many stanzas does the poem have?

_____

2. Look at the first stanza. What is the rhyming pattern?

    a. AABB

    b. ABAB

    c. ABBA

3. What is this poem about?

_____

4. What is the poem asking you to do?

_____

5. Who does the "I" refer to?

_____

6. What title would you give this poem?

_____

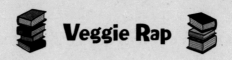

Veggie Rap

In *Ms. Hall Is a Goofball!*, Mr. Hynde tries to convince the Ella Mentry students to eat vegetables. Read Mr. Hynde's rap.

You say tomatoes. Well, so do I.

I'd rather eat tomatoes than apple pie.

All the teens like to eat their greens,

and my favorite one is lima beans.

I like dill and I always will.

You'll never fail if you eat kale.

I'll always finish my plate of spinach.

Black-eyed peas, if you please.

I'll take a glass of that wheat grass.

I got no stress when I eat watercress.

Only a bumpkin don't love pumpkin.

Cauliflower gives me the power.

Nothing faddish about eating a radish.

Don't be a weenie. Just eat a zucchini.

I won't hustle unless my sprouts are Brussels.

I hope you won't shriek when I take a leek.

I'm not joking, I'm artichoking.

A Fine Line

In the previous Party Pooper rap, the last words of many of the lines rhymed. This vegetable rap has a different rhyming pattern. Throughout most of the rap, the rhyming words are within the same line. This is called **internal rhyme**.

Directions: In the spaces below, or on a separate sheet of paper, try out these exercises.

1. Write five of the rhyming word pairs that occur within the same line. We've given you one example to get you started.

    teens   +   greens

_____+_____

_____+_____

_____+_____

_____+_____

2. Complete the lines of the rap so that they contain internal rhymes.

a. Be smarter not _____; eat a cucumber.

b. No, I won't share it! Don't eat from my _____.

3. Choose one of the vegetables from the box. Write a line of poetry using internal rhyme in which another word rhymes with the vegetable.

_____

_____

 Reading tip from Andrea: If you're a little confused by a page or a chapter, read it over again before going further. It will slow you down, of course, but repeating the material helps you remember it.

Rhyme Time!

Different letters and pairs of letters can represent the same sound. For example, "school" and "rule" rhyme because the **oo** in "school" and the **u** in "rule" make the same sound.

Directions: In the space provided or on a separate sheet of paper, fill in the blanks with the correct letter pairs from the box to complete the book titles. Remember that the My Weird School titles always rhyme!

in   oo   ai   et   ey   io   er   ou

1. Miss Klute Is a H____t!

2. Mr. Hynde Is Out of His M____d!

3. Mrs. M____er Is on Fire!

4. Mrs. Lane Is a P____n!

5. Mr. Granite Is from Another Plan____!

6. Coach Hyatt Is a R____t!

7. Mr. Burke Is B____serk!

8. Mayor Hubble Is in Tr____ble!

Conclusion

The Movie in Your Head

Here's the bottom line.* Reading can take you to a different world.

Did you ever get so absorbed watching a movie or playing a video game that you lost track of the time? I think we've all had that experience. You forget about everything else in your life for a little while. You forget about that homework you needed to do, or that test you had to study for. You forget about that mean kid

---

*Did you ever notice that "the bottom line" is never on the bottom line? What's up with that?

at school who said that horrible thing to you on the playground.

It's a nice feeling to get lost in a movie or video game, isn't it? Books can give you that same feeling. My goal with My Weird School is to create a story that's so fun and captivating, you'll start reading it, and an hour or two later you'll look up and feel like you weren't reading at *all*. It felt like you were watching a movie in your head.

I hope that when you "graduate" from My Weird School, you'll want to read books by other authors. I can't guarantee that *every* book is going to be as much fun as a My Weird School book, but as reading becomes easier for you, you're going to enjoy it more. You're going to get better at it. And at some point, you're going to see that movie in your head, trust me.

Answer Key

Chapter 1

ALL ABOUT SUBS

1. a

2. sick

3. work

4. comic book

5. unicycle

JUST FOR LAUGHS

1. yes

2. yes

3. no

4. yes

GROSS AND MYSTERIOUS

Answers will vary.

Chapter 2
SUM IT UP!

(Answers may vary.) Mr. Burke and Mr. Klutz had a lawn mower race. Mr. Klutz won. A.J. and his friends think both school staff members are weird. The students think Mr. Burke may be hiding a secret.

SUM UP THE SUMMARY

(Answers may vary.) Mr. Burke and Mr. Klutz have a lawn mower race. The students think Mr. Burke may be hiding something.

JUST DESERTS

1. rain

2. snow

3. continents

4. Antarctica

5. Sahara

6. sand

A LITTLE BIT SHORTER NOW

(Answers may vary.) Deserts are places on land that get less than ten inches of rain or snow in a year. They vary in temperature and terrain.

Chapter 3
COLLECTING THE EVIDENCE

1. *Mrs. Meyer Is on Fire!*

2. banner

3. candles

4. weirdest

5. fire station

MAKING PREDICTIONS

1. yes

2. no

3. yes

4. no

WHAT COMES NEXT

1. c

Chapter 4

GLUE'S CLUES

1. c

ON PINS AND NEEDLES

1. b
2. a
3. a
4. a

HOMOPHONES AND HOMOGRAPHS

1. a
2. b
3. b
4. a
5. a
6. b
7. b

8. b

9. b

Chapter 5

MR. VENN IS AN ALIEN

Andrea   both   A.J.

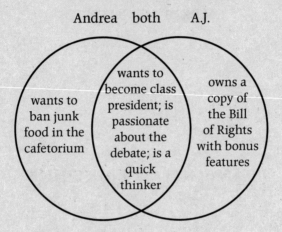

wants to ban junk food in the cafetorium

wants to become class president; is passionate about the debate; is a quick thinker

owns a copy of the Bill of Rights with bonus features

TEAM ANDREA OR TEAM A.J.?

Answers will vary.

WEIRD IN OPPOSITE WAYS

(Answers may vary.)

1. Mr. Cooper dresses up as superhero experts to explain each subject.

2. Miss Daisy pretends not to know anything so that students will have to explain what they know about math.

3. Mr. Cooper teaches what he knows, but Miss Daisy lets her class teach what they know.

4. They both make learning fun. Or both are weird.

MAKE YOUR OWN TEACHER

Answers will vary.

Chapter 6
BREAKING NEWS

1. d	3. c	5. e
2. f	4. a	6. b

WHAT TO DO IN A HABOOB

Cause	Effect
"Cover your faces!" yelled Miss Newman.	"I got it," I yelled as I picked up the camera.
Finally, the haboob blew past us.	I pulled my T-shirt over my face to keep the sand away.
"Grab the camera off the floor," Miss Newman yelled.	The sky got calm.
She kissed me!	"When are you gonna get married?" asked Michael.

Chapter 7

JURASSIC FACTS AND DINO-PINIONS

1. I
2. I
3. F
4. O

A MILLION HUNDRED HYPERBOLES

The most boring thing in the history of the

world

I thought I was gonna die.

After a million hundred hours

Just about every kind of candy in the world was

there.

You'll never believe in a million hundred years

Bonus: Answer will vary.

Chapter 8

CAN YOU EXPAND ON THAT?

1. and

2. but

3. and

4. because

5. or

6. and

COMPOUND SUBJECTS AND PREDICATES

1. Mr. Cooper pulled out his math textbook and told the class to turn to page twenty-three.

2. Emily turned around, leaned in, and whispered a secret to Andrea.

3. Alexia took the class pet home but forgot to feed him.

4. The students and teachers are ready for summer vacation.

5. Andrea, Alexia, and Pierre wanted to see the *Mona Lisa* in Paris.

6. Ryan or Neil can take the library book home tonight.

ALPHABET SOUP

Answers will vary.

SIMPLIFY, SIMPLIFY, SIMPLIFY

1. My name is A.J. and I hate snot.

2. Ms. Kraft ran.

3. Mr. Cooper wears a cape.

Chapter 9
RYAN GETS HIS SAY

1. c

2. b

3. c

4. d

5. b

EVERYBODY LOVES ANDREA

Answers will vary.

Chapter 10
A PICTURE IS WORTH A MILLION HUNDRED WORDS

1. Andrea: angry

2. Ryan: happy

3. Michael: happy

4. A.J. is reading something that makes Andrea mad.

A BIG CHECK

1. Ella Mentry

2. Ella Mentry

3. Ella Mentry

4. Ella Mentry is making a donation to the school.

A SCENE FROM THE VOMITORIUM

Details may include a cafeteria table, peanut butter and jelly sandwiches, A.J., Alexia, Ryan, Michael, and Neil, and milk coming out of Neil's nose.

Chapter II
PARTY POOPER POETRY

1. 5
2. a
3. The poem is about how great the Party Pooper is.
4. Buy a Party Pooper.
5. Mr. Hynde
6. Answer will vary.

VEGGIE RAP

1. Any of the following:

    teens, greens

    dill, will

    fail, kale

    finish, spinach

    peas, please

    glass, grass

    stress, watercress

    bumpkin, pumpkin

    cauliflower, power

    faddish, radish

    weenie, zucchini

    hustle, Brussels

    shriek, leek

    joking, artichoking

2. a. dumber

    b. carrot

3. Answers will vary.

RHYME TIME

1. oo

2. in

3. ey

4. ai

5. et

6. io

7. er

8. ou